Jon Scieszka's TRUCKTOWN

Help! I Am Wet!

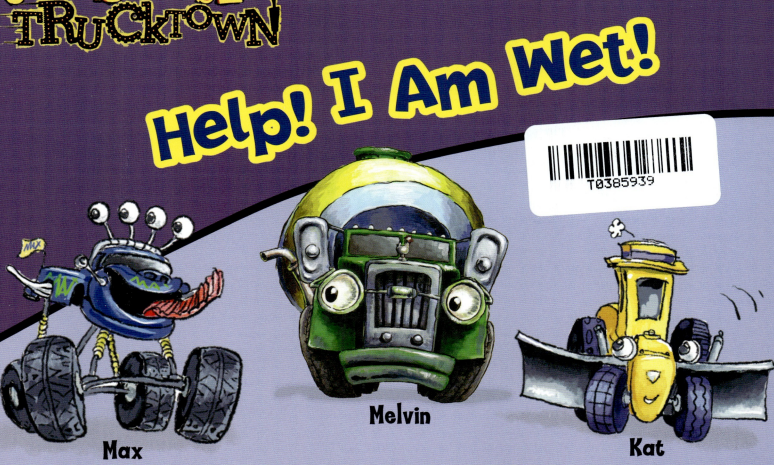

Max

Melvin

Kat

Adapted by Alison Hawes

Illustrated by dESiGN garage

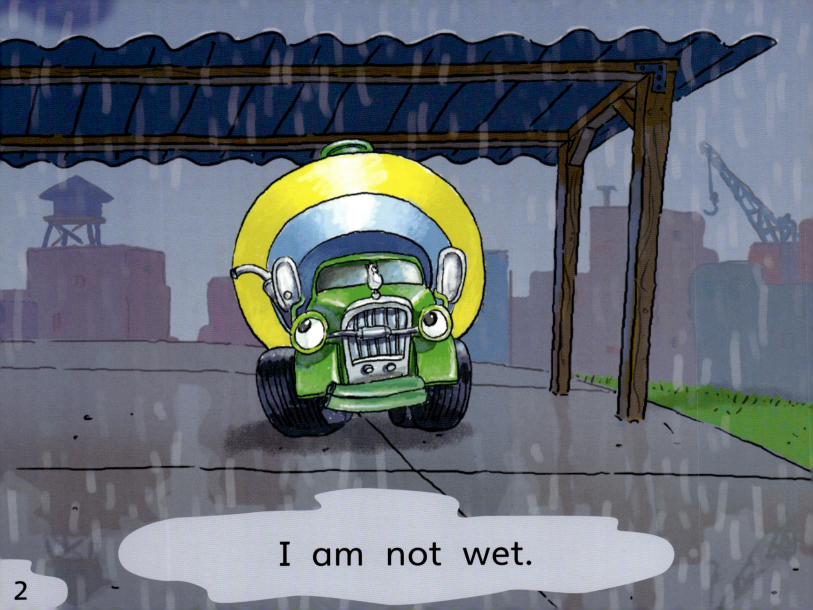

I am not wet.

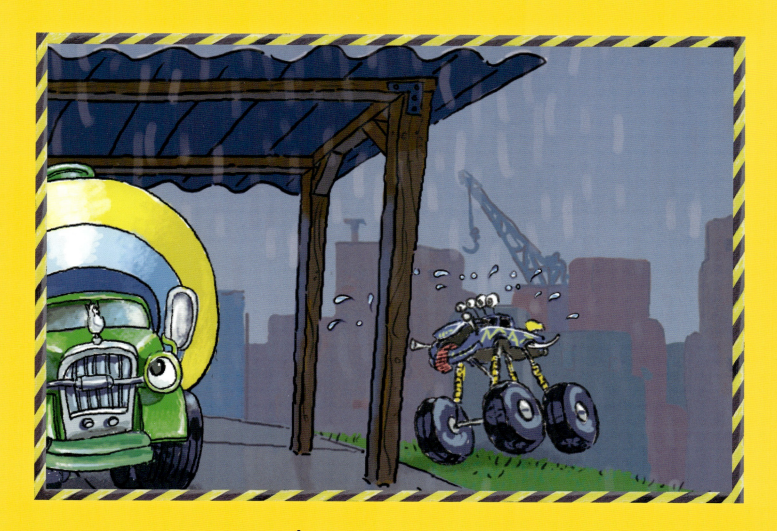

Help! I am wet.

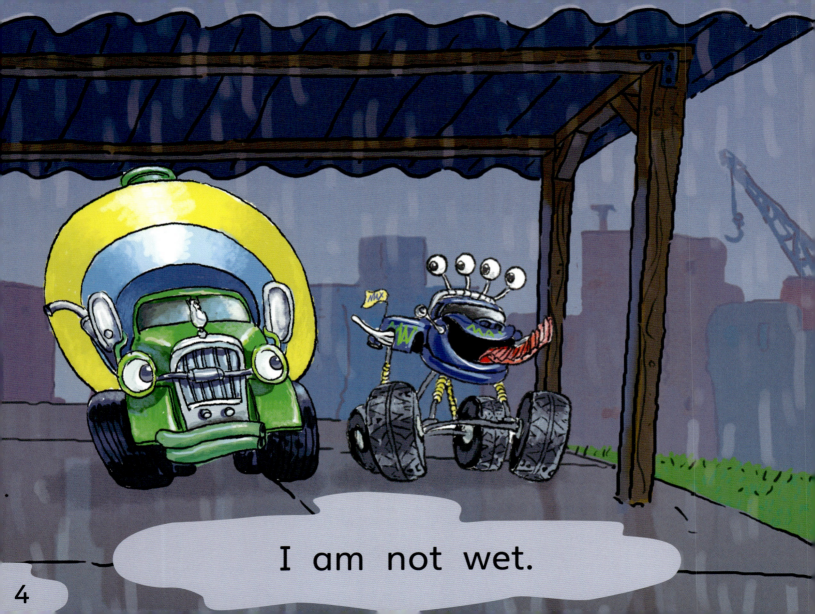

I am not wet.

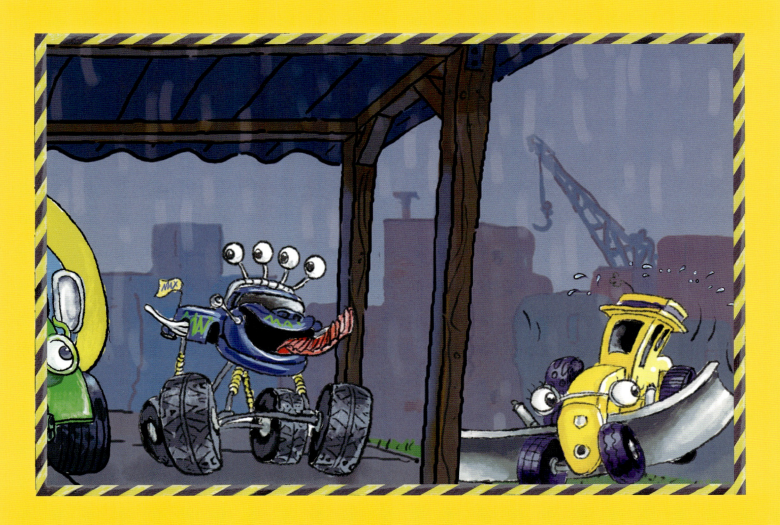

Help! I am wet.

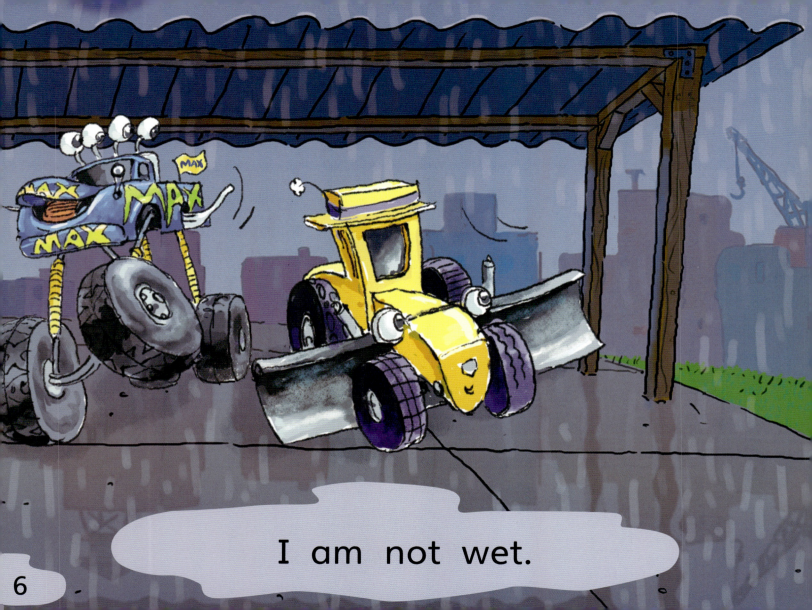

I am not wet.

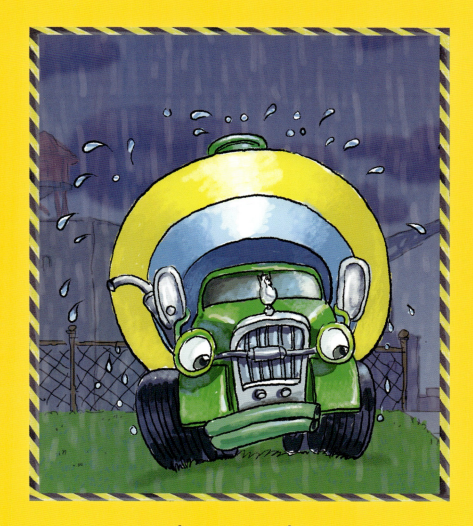

Help! Help!

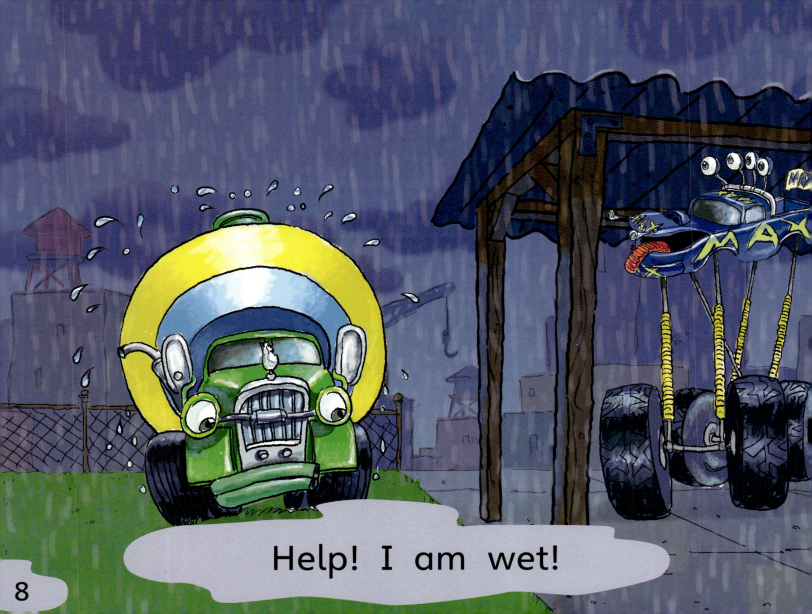

Help! I am wet!